The Official Guide to Building a Referral-Based Business

The Official Guide to Building a Referral-Based Business

Cezar Mansour

Beach Press

First Edition

Copyright © 2004 by Cezar Mansour. Printed and bound in the United States of America. All rights reserved, including the right of reproduction in whole or in part in any form.

Although the author and the publisher have made every effort to ensure the accuracy and the completeness of information contained in this book, we assume no responsibility for errors, inaccuracies, omissions or any inconsistency herein. Any slights of people, places, or organizations are unintentional.

Published by Beach Press
Manufactured in the United States of America
ISBN: 0-9754891-0-0
Library of Congress Control Number: 2004105356

Cover design by Bree Montanarello

Dedication

To all my family and friends, especially to my wife Tiffany and my three children.

Special thanks to Larry Ineno, without your patience and commitment this book wouldn't have been possible.

Additional thanks to Bree Montanarello for your work on the cover design and to Brad Nelson for taking the time to edit this book.

Table of Contents

Introduction: Unplugging Yourself From the Matrix

A couple of years back my family was comfortable but somewhat restless. I was supporting my wife and three children by working for one of the largest automotive corporations in the world. A year later, we were sinking under so much debt that I had to use my mom's credit cards to keep us afloat…and this all took place because of what I set out to do.

When I started my own business, I knew what I was leaving. My job in corporate America gave me a stable paycheck, a solid retirement package, and healthcare benefits that protected my entire family.

I didn't take the decision to leave my job lightly. After all, my wife and three young children were counting on my support. Before I resigned I planned, saved, and did everything I could to make sure I was making the right choice. Unfortunately, all the goal setting in the world wasn't enough to prepare me for the challenge ahead.

The few months after leaving my job were the most intense times I have ever faced. Establishing my business involved spending all the money I had, and having to trust that the returns would come later. At one point, all my credit cards were maxed-out, my 401(k) was liquidated, and I was two months behind on my car payment, mortgage, rent, and utilities—not to mention the daily expenses that came with three kids.

Finally, after all my financial resources were drained, my mother stepped in. She offered to help build my business the only way she could—with her credit cards. I reluctantly accepted her generosity and ended up maxing out her cards too. And just when things seemed like they couldn't get worse…

The phone call came from a general manager in the company where I worked. "Would you like to come back and work for us?" Then offers from other automotive companies came as well. The calls were both a temptation and an ego booster during some pretty low times. I began thinking that if I went back, I would have the safety and security again; I would have a paycheck within three weeks and another one—all on exactly the same day, every month.

During these times in my new career, the allure of returning to the comfort of my past was so strong it literally called me on the phone. At the same time, I realized that working for someone else meant that my focus and determination would be gone.

So instead of thinking about going back to the safety of corporate life, I considered the worst-case scenario. If I had to make extra money, if things reached a point where I had no choice but to get a job, I'd pick up my toolbox and find work doing what I had done in my early twenties. I would fix cars again at $10-$20 an hour. It wouldn't be fun but I would choose that over returning to full-time corporate work.

Don't get me wrong, the pull to take the offers that were coming in were strong. After all, I liked my job. I left on good terms. The company liked my work, they paid me a decent salary, and gave me the tools to work effectively.

On the other hand, during my nearly 10 years at the company, I was frustrated. I felt like I wasn't in control of my time. No matter how high I moved up, I knew I would always have to report to my supervisor about my daily progress.

Throughout the office, I wondered why so many employees, including myself, allowed our self-worth to be determined by the evaluations of our superiors, when deep down we knew that we tried our best and did a great job.

Across corporate America, good employees work hard and take pride in what they do. Career-driven people push themselves ahead. They want to be recognized by their bosses because moving up in a company has everything to do with how their supervisors view their work.

My classic case of workplace frustration went as follows: I would walk down the hallway and see my supervisor or his boss. If either of them smiled and greeted me with "Hey Cezar, how's your day going?" it would be a great day for me. I would feel like my work was appreciated.

If, however, we were walking past each other and my supervisor didn't even look my way, I would feel unappreciated, or maybe that I wasn't doing a good enough job. I was constantly concerned about how he felt about me because his beliefs were what would lead to a promotion.

Inside, I was convinced that my supervisors were just like me. We all were probably preoccupied with similar matters: What we needed to get done that day, how we were going to get it done, and what our bosses were thinking about us. At the same time, I couldn't help but feel that the work I was doing was connected with the mood of my boss or his boss. I learned some valuable lessons about corporate culture. The world of big business focuses on making workers as productive as possible. But no matter how hard a company pushes its employees, there are always those who work harder than others. So how do businesses deal with this?

They whip the fastest horse while the slow ones are allowed to graze. They never allow the most productive and effective employees to sit back like the ones who are there to graze. In fact, if you produce top results they demand more from you; while they continue to require less from those who don't work as hard. The worst part is, both the motivated and the unmotivated often get paid the same amount.

Why I Chose to Stay the Course

If I spent three months coaching my daughter's soccer team I would spend time with her and meet other committed parents. And in the process I could create business contacts that would ultimately lead to a transaction (total time commitment: six to eight hours per week).

One transaction within three months could earn me up to $3,600. On the other hand, I could get a part-time job making $10 an hour for 30 hours a week, which would give me the $3,600 within the same three months. I realized that you couldn't support a family of five with that kind of income.

What would happen if, in addition to coaching soccer, I participated in a networking group and the local chamber of commerce as well? Now, if I gained one client every three months from all three activities, I would earn $10,800.

Instead of working by someone else's schedule, like I was at a company, I would work on my own time. Which in this case meant coaching my daughter's soccer team and meeting other motivated people.

Devoting Time to Develop Your Business

As you'll read throughout the pages of this book, successful networking can be summed up in three words: Socialize, socialize, socialize. Keep in mind that this takes time. Building a strong client base takes months and years of hard work.

I'm not suggesting that you quit your well-paying, stable job and open up your own business. In fact, owning your own company is one of the most stressful careers you can have. Dealing with workers comp, licensing, rent, healthcare benefits, and insurance never makes the list of "The Top Things That Made You Want to Have Your Own Business." What I do believe is that self-employment as an independent contractor, or anyone who works by referral, is about the most rewarding work you can do.

Since leaving my job, I have more time to spend with my family and friends. I am able to do things that I never could before, like coach my daughter's soccer teams, watch the kids so my wife can take a break from full-time motherhood, pick my kids up after school, and just hang out with friends.

I am able to decide when I'll show up at the office, when I'll take lunch, and who I'll meet that day. If I'm feeling motivated I can work till 2:00 in the morning. If want to hang out with a friend, I can spend three hours with him during lunch. I am rewarded directly for the amount of effort I put into my business.

Giving You a Plan of Action

When I began my business, I found lots of great resources on how to set goals, how to get clients, and the legal aspects of establishing a company. Unfortunately, I couldn't find books that addressed *how to start* a referral-based business, from setting up my office to contacting clients.

My goal is to give you a comprehensive overview of everything you need to know to get your business off to a solid start. If you put 75 percent of this book into action it will lead to less stress and worry as you build your business.

When you are self-employed you are not paid by the hour or by a salary. Instead, you're paid per job or project. When your project is complete, you stop getting paid. It's up to you to find more projects.

As a self-employed person, no one is keeping track of your hours. No one needs to, since the time you're in the office is irrelevant. What is important is how effective you are at gaining new clients and staying in contact with the one's you've worked with before.

If you've chosen an industry where you have to develop your own clientele and maintain repeat business such as: a mortgage broker, real estate agent, doctor, hair stylist, lawyer, or financial planner, this book is for you.

It is a good man who learns from his mistakes. It is a wise man who learns from the mistakes of others.

What I present in these pages is everything I've learned along the way. Yes, you can learn by trial and error. That, however, can be very expensive. Whenever possible, it's better to learn from someone else's mistakes. This book will put you ahead of the game.

For instance, in the beginning I spent thousands of dollars on print ads, fliers, and everything else that people say you must have in order to promote yourself. Unfortunately, the money I invested didn't bring in business. Later, I learned that creating solid relationships and treating people well were the keys to making my business grow.

A couple of years ago, I saw the film *The Matrix.* In it, Keanu Reaves's character, Neo, was someone who was unsatisfied with life. He wanted more out his existence and questioned matters that few took the time to think about. He was willing to make the sacrifices to find the answers he was looking for.

Ultimately, his decision to look for the truth required him to unplug himself from "the Matrix"—the computer-generated reality that everyone else was connected to. The process of unplugging himself came with a tremendous amount pain and struggle. Like Neo, when you set out to work for yourself, you have to unplug from the company or employer, the steady work, and the regular paycheck.

No one is going to feed you anymore. You're not going to be handed anything. I believe that all people who set out on their own have to go through a process of "unplugging themselves from the Matrix." In other words, all self-employed people have to decide what sacrifices they are willing to make. What are they willing to do in order to stop working for someone else and start working for themselves?
The decision is not easy and the journey is even more difficult—especially at the beginning. But in the end, I

believe that it is worth every ounce of stress and anxiety that comes along. The moment you are free to be your own boss, set your own path, and decide how successful you want to be, is one of the most fulfilling experiences you can have.

The reality is, you don't have to be well connected and you don't have to have your new business venture running through the veins of your ancestors. What you need is the courage to stay the course.

The tools provided in this book, along with every last drop of focus and determination you have, will put you in the ranks of millions of others who—everyday—successfully work by referral.

Chapter 1
Welcome to the Freedom and Fulfillment You've Been Looking For. Now Get to Work

Self-employment is a dream that many have but few attain. The allure makes perfect sense. Who wouldn't want to set his own hours, work when he wished, and get paid well for his efforts? Unfortunately, like most desirable things in life, self-employment comes at a price. After all, if it were easy then we all would be entrepreneurs or independent contractors. What it takes to work on your own is determination and complete focus. And after all the heartache, the rewards of success will come.

The driving force behind what you will read in this book comes from what I've learned along the way. Read the next pages carefully, follow the steps and tips, and you'll be ahead of about 90 percent of your colleagues. So let's get started on the path to joining the growing number of people who—just like you—find success in working for themselves.

Which Phase is Your Business In?

If you've chosen an industry where you have to develop your own clientele and maintain repeat business such as a mortgage broker, real estate agent, doctor, hair stylist, lawyer, or financial planner, this book is for you.

In the process of building your referral-based business, you will most likely fit into two categories:

1. You've just begun working by referral.
2. You've been working by referral and wish to continue meeting goals and grow.

Read the following two sections and decide which phase resembles your business most.

Phase 1. The Beginning: Stay the Course

Mark recently quit his job at a prominent financial services firm. A month ago, he started working as an independent contractor for a local mortgage company.

After a few frustrating weeks, the initial excitement and drive that pushed him to pass his real-estate exam and quit his well-paying corporate job fizzled away.

The bills were piling up, his rent was due, and the phone sat silently on his desk. Mark was concerned that he had made the wrong choice. He was second-guessing his decision to leave the company.

Thoughts like these began to run through his mind daily:
"What was I thinking? I was making good money. Sure, the hours were frustrating and I wasn't getting paid what I deserved. But all that beats the stress I feel now."

He was now contemplating returning to his old job or at least finding another one at a competing firm. At this point, he decided to schedule a meeting with his boss to share his frustrations. Tricia, the owner of the mortgage firm, invited Mark into her office. As usual she was gracious and warm.

"Mark, how are things? Lately, I've noticed that you seem preoccupied. Is there anything I can help you with?"

"Well, I've been thinking hard about things. I decided that I needed to talk you, and that I needed to be honest about what I'm going through right now."

Tricia gets up from her desk and offers him some coffee.

"Does this have to do with business here?" she asks.

"Yeah it does. I've been here two months, and I'm afraid that I'm not cut out for this. I mean, quitting my last job felt like such a good move. But now I feel like it was a big mistake." He takes a sip of coffee.

"I know *exactly* how you feel." Her words surprise Mark. He didn't expect his boss to say this.

"What do you mean? Your office is beautiful, your business keeps growing and…"

"Do you think this happened overnight? Listen, there were many months in the beginning where I wondered what the heck I was doing. And then, when I felt like giving up, someone came and told me exactly what I needed to hear. Do you want to know what it was?"

"Of course," he says.

"I'm glad to hear that. Remember these words: *Trust yourself and socialize with friends,"* she says.
"I'm sorry. Can you explain what that means?" asks Mark.

"Think about it. It's during the most difficult times, the times when you least want to, that you have to depend on yourself and push yourself ahead. Success is often just around the corner, you just don't see it. Sadly, that's when most people give up. I've seen it too many times." She pauses and takes a sip from her mug.

Mark doesn't feel like she understands what he's going through.

"Now, I know that *trust yourself and socialize with friends* may seem too simple right now, but answer this question for me: Why did you quit your job?" she asks.

"I felt like I wasn't being rewarded for my work. I was driving myself crazy trying to meet deadlines and demands from my boss. Meanwhile, other people seemed to have all the free time in the world. I started thinking: Why am I working so hard to make the same amount of money as people who push themselves less than me?" he says.

"Good. Now answer this one. Why did you choose this job? After all, you could have gotten a similar job at another company, right?" she asks.

"Yeah. I guess you're right. I had the experience. I could've easily found another job, for maybe even more pay somewhere else. I just thought that I would run into the same kinds of problems," he responds.

"Sounds good so far. Next question: Why did you choose to become an independent contractor, instead of working for a major corporation?" she asks.

"Well, after about a year at the company, I noticed that I had a certain drive that my colleagues didn't. I would take on tasks that other people avoided.

"I got along with my colleagues and supervisors, even the ones people said were tough to work with...you know, the ones that are known to get mad all the time and expect way too much. I felt like I had good communication skills yet I wasn't being rewarded for my efforts and…"

Tricia interrupts him.

"Let me tell you what I just heard. When you came into my office five minutes ago, you were frustrated and fed up. How do you feel now?" she asks.

"I feel relieved…I'm glad that I'm not at that office anymore."

"I can tell. Wouldn't you say that you're at a better place now than you were last year?" she asks.

"You're right. I'm so glad to be out of that place," he says.

"And you should be, it obviously wasn't your dream job," she says.

"No, that's for sure. But that's why I'm so disappointed. I'm glad that I'm not at my old job anymore, but I know that once I leave your office, I'll feel stressed out again."

"Of course. But now you've reminded yourself why you're here. You know that deep down, you have the drive and energy to make this happen.
"Sure, your skills aren't all there yet. This is brand new for you. But remember what I told you: *Trust yourself and socialize*."

"Help me understand what you mean by this," he says.

"Think about it. If it were easy, this whole self-employment thing, then everyone would be doing it. After all, who really wants to work for someone who tells her what to do? I'm sure that almost everyone wishes that they were their own boss.
"You have what it takes. It's there. You just need to regain focus and remind yourself of your goals," she says.

"But what do I do from here?" he asks.

"For most, it takes one or two low points for them to open up and take advice. I know that you're now ready to move to the next level," she says.

"How?"

"Lucky for you, I've made all the mistakes already. I've had all the sleepless nights. Follow the steps that I've learned along the way and you'll avoid the pitfalls and get the results that you've been looking for."

Tricia pulls out a thick white binder. She places it in front of Mark.

"These are the things I've learned over the years. In these pages is the history of my business. What I did right and wrong, and what I think is the most important information you need to get going in the right direction."

"You mean you've actually taken time to write everything down—the mistakes and the accomplishments?" he asks.

"It's the only way I could avoid making the same mistakes again. When you read through this book you'll see what I've gone through and what I've learned. Your ambition and drive—and I know you have it—combined with what's in these pages, will virtually guarantee your success," she says.

Mark takes the notebook and says, "If this book has the answers, I can't wait to find out what they are."

"Tell you what. Let's meet every week and see how you're doing. That way you can ask me questions and tell me what you're going through," she says.

"Are you sure? You're not too busy?" he asks.

"Step one in the notebook is *put relationships first*. Think of it this way. Your success is good for you and good for me. Our relationship is what counts and I know you have what it takes to succeed," she says.

Mark gets up and walks towards the door, white notebook under his arm. "Thanks so much Tricia, I can't wait to meet next time," he says.

"Me too," she responds, "…me too."

Phase 2. Business is Growing: The Next Step

Rose Jackson started her financial planning career four years ago. After her children were school age, Rose and her husband decided that if she returned to work, their family would have more money to save for their children's college educations.

She spent about a year and a half networking, making phone calls, sending e-mails, and basically sharing about her business to anyone who would listen. She worked hard to get her client base to a point where she was making a good income.

Presently, she is in her fourth year and she has succeeded in meeting her goal of gaining a new client every two months. Things are moving in an exciting direction. Almost 90 percent of her new clients are people that came to her as a referral from a friend, colleague, or family member.

As her business grows and her family responsibilities change, Rose is getting busier and busier. Recently, she has felt overwhelmed. She's unable to keep up with the constant client contact required for any referral-based business to grow.

Rose is at a crossroads. Business is fantastic. Unfortunately, she is unable to stay on top of contacting her friends and clients from the past.

At this point, she needs to implement a system of regular and consistent communication with her friends, family, and clients. Focusing only on new clients will cause her to lose valuable business. By neglecting her past clients, Rose is making the most common mistake of a person who works by referral.

Review

Phase 1: Mark is just starting out. He has bills piling up, but no money or business coming in.

Must do's: Organize and socialize

If Phase 1 resembles your current business status, first, you need to organize yourself for the steady stream of clientele you expect to have (i.e. filing cabinet, desk, and contacts).

Once you're organized, it's time to *socialize, socialize, socialize,* which means going to parties, family events, or local business networking groups. Your goal is to meet people and develop relationships.

Phase 2: Rose has been in business for four years. She's making a good income and has plenty of business. But the level of service that she is accustomed to giving her clients has decreased because she is too busy.

She needs to improve her organizational skills. She needs to implement systems to keep in contact with current and previous clients. Otherwise, she'll risk losing her constant flow of repeat business.

Must do's: Consistent organization and a system of keeping in touch

If Phase 2 resembles your business, congratulations, you're off to a good start. Now, you need to improve your organizational skills and implement a system to keep in touch and thank your current and past clients.

Organization and Socialization Should Be Done Simultaneously

Always keep in mind that your organizing skills *and* your socializing skills work together. The more organized you are, the more time you'll have to meet people. As you read through this manual, you'll learn how to develop systems and strategies that will help you create a successful referral-based business.

Chapter 2
Get Organized Part 1: Your Success Depends on Your Ability to Organize

How many times have you or someone you know said, "If I just had an extra hour everyday to relax or get things done, life would be much easier." When you work smarter and set the right systems in place, extra time and a feeling of control are just around the corner.

Organization gives you the freedom to do what you enjoy. If you stay on top of the paperwork and e-mails, you'll find yourself with more than a few minutes of extra time. In fact, you may have hours to spend being a coach on your child's sports team, joining a networking group, working on a hobby, or just relaxing.

Most people desire the independence and flexibility that comes from being in control of their own time. What keeps this goal out of reach, however, is either the lack of self-motivation or organization. Remember, you're the one who is in control of your prosperity. You're the only one who will push yourself to stay organized…or keep yourself from being organized.

The following steps are critical to managing your time. They will save you stress, heartache, and will lead you to a good night's sleep and a feeling of self-control.

Organize First, Get Business Next

Filing paperwork, dealing with bills, and answering e-mails and phone calls, all at the same time is enough to make anybody feel overwhelmed and out of control.

The way you overcome these feelings is to take care of everything in a systematic way. Before responding to that first phone call or e-mail, everything around you needs to be within your control.

Think about your workday. It's filled with clients who need to be contacted, helped along, or reassured; people you need to meet with; and urgent matters that must be addressed. Meanwhile, the e-mails, letters, and bills will continue to pile up; pulling you away from dealing with things that bring in the paycheck—unless, of course, you have an organizational system that you adhere to.

Set aside time (it may take weeks) to accomplish the task of getting organized. It is key to getting your mind ready to receive everything that is out there for you. The time you invest from the beginning will reward you over and over.

The simple steps you take now will save you time and aggravation later. More importantly, not sticking to a system means losing focus, control, and most importantly, business.

Five Essentials for Your Office

Here are the top five must-haves for your office:

1. A roomy, dedicated space
2. Files and file cabinet
3. Computer

4. Phone with voicemail
5. A combination printer/fax/scanner/copier

All of these items seem pretty simple. But I'm continually surprised how many people neglect to start off with these basics. If you don't have these five essentials in your office, get them now. Remember, the more stable your foundation is, the better equipped you'll be to take on the challenges of the future.

1. Choose a Desk that Gives You Room to Work

Have a space dedicated to running your business and make sure it's big enough to work comfortably. This should not be the place where you pay the bills. This may seem trivial. But remember what I said before, setting up a referral-based business requires a different mindset. You are part of a select group of people. Establishing the career you always wanted is going to require you to dig into the deepest parts of who you are. So you have to create a space where your focus is completely on work.

2. Files and a File Cabinet Keep the Paperwork at Bay

All your bills, invoices, bank statements, and business documents need to be labeled and accounted for. Create a system where you are able to easily file the paperwork that you receive. Get all of your paperwork organized then file and label your folders. The time required to get this done depends on how much you have to organize as well as your work style.

3. If Your Computer is More than 2 1/2 Years Old—Maybe It's Time for a Change

If you don't have one already, or if you have one that is outdated, you need a new computer. What you should buy depends on your needs. With technology improving every day, almost any new computer will do the basics. And the best part is, prices just keep going down, while computers get more efficient.

Here's the software that you will need to get started: a word processor (like Microsoft Word or Word Perfect), a CRM (Customer Relationship Management software, like Microsoft Outlook or ACT), and a high-speed Internet connection like a cable modem or DSL. Don't skimp here. Time is money.

4. A Phone with Voice Mail Makes Clients Happy

Make sure that you're easily available to your clients. Even if they can't reach you directly, they need to know you are ready to meet their needs. So make sure you have some type of reliable voice mail system in place—one that you can access away from the office.

5. A Combination Printer/Fax/Scanner/Copier Saves Time and Money

This is the best way to maximize your office dollar. These machines are fantastic since they allow you to send and receive faxes, print documents, and scan images you need to send clients. If you are going to be printing high volumes of documents, then consider buying a used laser printer in addition to your combination printer. The laser printer will print documents quickly and the toner lasts a long time.

Once you have the five essentials for your office—your work space, files and file cabinet, computer, phone with voicemail, and a combination printer-fax-scanner-copier—you will have removed many of the barriers that keep you from working efficiently while you're there.

Five Tips to Making Your Office Run Smoothly

After you have filed your documents in a place that is neat and organized your desk is ready for business.

Now here are five essentials that will make paperwork and client contact a breeze:

1. Document filing system
2. Banking system
3. To-do list (daily and weekly)
4. Updated meeting calendar with personal appointments
5. CRM (Customer Relationship Management software, like Microsoft Outlook)

1. Your Document Filing System is Key to Keep Track of Your Spending

Start by making sense of the overwhelming amount of paperwork you need to manage. Then put all of it in one place. After you have all of your files together, you will need to organize them. First off, an 8x10 envelope for every month, will keep your receipts together. Keep in mind that you need to have a good handle on them since receipts document your losses and expenses.

Create separate envelopes for the following:

1. Auto (fuel and insurance)
2. Equipment (printer, fax, and computer)
3. Office Supplies (paper, bottled water, pens, and paperclips)
4. Insurance (business and health)
5. Utilities (gas, electric, and water)

You may need to create more envelopes or less, depending on your business.

If you have never done this before, it will definitely take time. The work will be well worth it. After a few months of keeping track of your records you will be able to assess your business's spending habits with clarity and certainty. For instance, if you look through your "Office Supplies" envelope you will see how much you spend on paper, ink for your printer, mailings, etc. Thus giving you immediate access to the information that will help you decide how to budget, cut costs, and save money.

2. Banking System

Set up an online bank account. This will save you time and postage. (You can't do this if your computer is not Internet-ready—yet another reason to invest in a machine that will make your life easier.).

Make sure you keep track of your current bank statements. Set up a time each month to reconcile your accounts and stay on top of your finances. Doing this will let you know how much more or less you need to work, how many hours you will need put in, and how many more phone calls you have to take care of to keep your business running smoothly. Most importantly, you will have a feeling of control over your business.

3. Daily To-Do-List

The goal of a to-do list is to guide you in completing specific tasks. Your to-do list should begin with tasks that you didn't finish the previous day. Once you're caught up, you'll be ready to tackle what needs to get done today. On the other hand, if you continue to put matters off, you'll find the tasks piling up on each other, which will eventually lead to missed deadlines and frustration.

Prioritization is key. Ask yourself the following questions: What needs to happen this morning? What needs to happen today? What can wait till tomorrow? What can wait till next week? And what can wait till next month?

Decide what needs to be addressed first. Getting these out of the way will enable you to be ready to handle any urgent matters that may arise.

4. Updated Monthly Calendar

What events take place every month? Some examples are clients whom you meet with on a regular basis, networking meetings, family gatherings, personal matters, and contacts that are made consistently. These types of recurring events should automatically go on your calendar.

5. CRM's Are Your Biggest Business Ally

Imagine with the click of a mouse being able to track all contacts you made with a specific client for this year and every year since you began working with him or her. You can do all of this through your CRM (Customer Relationship Management) software, which manages your e-mail.

Unfortunately, too many people think that e-mail is a burden. These people often wish for the days when phone messages and First Class letters were the norm. But anyone who has a pulse and a business they want to grow must realize that e-mail is here to stay. If you have doubts, just ask the United States Postal Service.

If you create an organized system for managing your messages, e-mail becomes a powerful tool. Once you have your system in place, I am certain that even the most e-mail-wary person will feel like it is technology worth getting used to. There are many kinds of organizational software available: ACT, Outlook, Prizm, and Franklin-Covey organizers to name some.

Think of CRM's, or Customer Relationship Management software, as exercise equipment. Just as there are multiple brands of software available, there are countless ways to stay fit. If a person is health conscious and works out every day doing calisthenics while someone else belongs to the best gym in the area but never exercises, who is healthier? In Chapter 3: Get Organized Part 2, I will specifically address this point. For now, deciding which is best for you depends on answering the question: What program will I use consistently?

Many people make the mistake of buying expensive software, thinking that the latest program will make them more organized. But the truth is, as with any software program, you must invest time learning about it, input contact information, then update it regularly.

Review

Follow These Steps and You're Way Ahead of the Game

Remember the five must-haves for your office:

1. A roomy, dedicated space
2. Files and file cabinet
3. Computer
4. Phone with voicemail
5. A combination printer/fax/scanner/copier

Followed by the five essentials to stay organized:

1. Document filing system
2. Banking system
3. To-do list (daily and weekly)
4. Updated meeting calendar with personal appointments
5. CRM (Customer Relationship Management software, like Microsoft Outlook)

Remember, if you invest the time in following these steps—and I won't kid you, it will take time—you're ahead of about 90 percent of those who are doing what you do. You will avoid the headaches that most people starting off go through, and you will set yourself up to meet and exceed your goals. You are giving yourself exactly what you need to stay the course and succeed.

Now in the next section, I'll take you step-by-step through your CRM and give you tips on staying organized.

Chapter 3
Get Organized Part 2: Exercise Equipment and the Ins of Outlook

Brian goes to his annual physical. His doctor tells him that he is 15 pounds over the target weight for someone his age and height. His doctor recommends that he lose the weight through regular exercise.

A few days after his physical, Brian drives by Fitness Express, a nearby gym, and decides to join. He begins a four-day per week exercise program. After a month of consistently walking on the treadmill, lifting weights, and swimming, he is excited about the weight he has lost. He's feeling better and looking better.

After a few weeks, however, he loses focus. Work gets busy and family responsibilities increase. Within a matter of months, these things take priority and he doesn't make time to go to the gym.

Brian continues to pay his monthly membership because he wants to lose weight and stay fit. Unfortunately, given his lack of focus and commitment, he has wasted his money and time.

Why does he, like most Americans who are trying to lose weight, struggle? Because the habits are not in place. He should have approached the matter by asking questions like, "How committed am I really going to be?" and, "Am I going to exercise no matter what? Am I willing to lose the weight even if I don't have the luxury of a gym membership?"

After all, no gym can motivate a person who is unorganized and uncertain about what he wants, at least over the long term. Once he asked the right questions, he could now proceed to take the necessary steps to reach his goals.

Many people new to the referral-based profession are like Brian. They have good intentions—they buy the right equipment and spend time getting organized—but they fail before they start. They don't fully appreciate the commitment that it takes to stay organized. It is an on-going daily task that increases as you become successful.

When you are setting out to get organized think of how you can avoid the struggle and heartache that most people go through. Carefully decide which CRM software (Customer Relationship Management) you'll use. No matter how much you spend on it, it's a waste of money if it's unused. A notebook organizer—like a Day Runner, written in daily—is far more effective than the latest CRM that sits in a computer without being opened up.

That's why I recommend Microsoft Outlook. It's simple and inexpensive. There are more sophisticated programs you can own. But all the technology you buy is meaningless if you don't use it. I like Outlook because it's widely available, user friendly, and integrates with your e-mail and PDA (Personal Digital Assistant, like a Palm Pilot).

Once you've committed yourself to use a CRM and make it a daily part of your life, the following tips will help you organize the information stored in it. Although the directions that follow use Microsoft Outlook, the steps will apply to most CRM systems.

How to Use Outlook: It's Easier than You Think

Making Sense of Your Inbox

When you open up Outlook on your computer you will see a section for e-mail. Once you get on-line and a new message comes into the computer, it goes straight into this e-mail software.

Just like many people have a mailbox at work, all new messages go straight into the inbox of this e-mail program. The messages will remain in the inbox until you delete them. If you don't have a way to file your messages, they quickly pile up. In fact, within the inboxes of most of computer users today, sit hundreds of messages jumbled together in no particular order. This is no way to keep track of e-mails, especially if your paycheck counts on staying organized.

Let's say that you're on the phone with a client and she wants you to refer back to a message she sent you. If you have hundreds of messages in your inbox, it will take you a long time to find the specific one you're looking for. Fumbling through numerous messages when a client is waiting is an inefficient way to do business, and you certainly won't sound like a well-organized person over the phone. The most frustrating part is that deep down, you know you should have already found a way to make this e-mail you're looking for easy to find. This anxiety is only made worse now that you have someone waiting for you on the phone.

As your business grows you will also begin receiving more e-mails than you ever did before. In fact, you may receive hundreds of e-mails every week. How do you keep track of all of these messages? The same way you do when you get a new client or account—you create file folders for each of them.

Unfortunately, when Linda Simm's e-mail comes to you in your inbox, you can't just pull out a file folder and write "Linda Simms" at the top with a Sharpie marker. The good news is, it's quite easy to figure out how to file things in your e-mail. And once you do it, you can organize other computer documents the same way.

(If you understand Outlook or your current CRM well, skip this section and continue onto page 36 "When is the Best Time to Get Organized?")

Here's how it works in Outlook. For other software the process is similar. Remember to refer to the user's manual for specific details.

1. Open up Outlook and click on the word "Inbox." You're now at the e-mail part of your software. Most of the time you are directed to it automatically. If you are connected to the Internet, the computer should begin to retrieve new messages.

2. With the word "Inbox" highlighted, go to the word "File" at the top of your screen. Click on it and select the word "Folder."

3. Now select the word "New Folder." A "New Folder" dialogue box (a window that pops up on your screen) will appear.

4. In the name field type in a reference name for the folder you want to create. For instance, name your folder "New Accounts." This folder will hold all the messages and folders for your new accounts.

5. Next, create and name a folder for each client in your "New Accounts." Each folder inside the "New Accounts" is called a sub-folder. To do this, click on the "New Accounts" folder (the one you just created in step 4) and repeat the same steps that you did to create the "New Accounts" folder (steps one through four). After you have done this with several clients you will have created a file tree.

Now, every time you receive a message from client such as John Mason, you simply click and drag it into the "John Mason" sub-folder under the main folder "New Accounts." Your goal is to keep your inbox as empty as possible. Each time you open it, read messages, and file them away.

Track Your Progress Through Your File Tree

Every e-mail from John Mason for this year will go into his personal folder under the "New Accounts" folder. At this point, every current client will have a sub-folder under the "New Accounts" folder. And when you click on "New Accounts," you will see all the clients you've worked with this year.

Every year or quarter you will want to create a new folder. For instance, you can name a folder "Past Clients," or simply date each folder like "Accounts 2005," "Accounts 2006," etc.

Every year you have a new folder that contains your clients. The most encouraging part is that you can now track everyone you've served. You will be surprised and encouraged when you see how each year your client list grows.

You can also track which clients are new and which have continued from the previous year. This is a powerful way to see whom you need to contact. If you're not certain whether you have communicated with a person lately, all you have to do is look under the current year and click open her folder. You have a record of all e-mails you have sent her within the year.

Once you have gotten the hang of creating a file tree in Outlook, you can now do the same for all your computer documents. Follow the steps described above in your word processing software (such as Word or Word Perfect) and all the documents you type and receive will be filed neatly and ready to access whenever you need them—like when you have your client on the phone.

When is the Best Time to Get Organized?

The simple answer: When the office is closed. Why? Because during business hours, there are too many distractions. Think about your typical workday. You arrive at the office. You read your e-mails, listen to messages, and you have a mountain of paperwork waiting for you on your desk. If you work at home add the following distractions: pets, children, the television, and everything else that keeps you from getting work done.

That's why I suggest you get organized during your non-business hours when your clients aren't around. During the evening, after everyone else has called it a night, begin to sort out your files, go through your e-mails that need to be deleted or filed, and make sense of all the paperwork on your desk. On the other hand, you may work better in the morning before work.

Are there days when you'll be too tired to deal with the mountain of paperwork on your desk? Of course. But soon you'll realize how staying organized makes your life easier and keeps that mountain to nothing more than a few sheets of paper. If you stay focused you will create a habit of staying up-to-date with your paperwork and e-mails, which will free up more time to create new business.

Without some type of strong organizational system in place, the files will pile up on your desk and you will waste valuable time looking for paperwork and e-mails. You will become less productive and you will have a feeling of always being behind or out of control, which will affect your attitude and your availability to clients. In a referral-based business, giving your clients service that is beyond their expectations is a must.

Lack of Planning on Your Part, Doesn't Constitute an Emergency on My Part…

Usually someone who says something like this is called hard-nosed. This quote, however, is so biting because it is true.

Some say that there is no such thing as a crisis. They believe that crises are the result of not planning enough. You may not agree with this. At the same time, consider how many urgent situations that could have been avoided if things were planned ahead of time.

For instance, after years of experience in the real estate industry, most real estate agents can predict certain events that will occur during a property purchase. Experienced realtors will anticipate many things, from the amount of time it will take for a property to sell, to what type of home a buyer will be interested in. Through experience, they have the solutions to problems that may arise.

On the other hand, an inexperienced realtor doesn't plan ahead. He doesn't anticipate the possible twists and turns of a transaction. He may have waited for the last minute to have the home inspected and didn't expect the negative report on the property. Now he has two days instead of twenty to get the house up to spec. If he thought ahead he would have had weeks to resolve whatever came up. Now matters need to be taken care of within 48 hours—making it an emergency for everyone—as well as possibly damaging his reputation.

Here is another example that points to the importance of planning ahead.

A couple purchases a large property on a beautiful hill. The only known negative aspect of the property is that about every 30 years, the area has mudslides. The buyers are fully aware of this when they purchase the home. Before moving in, they plan to make sure that they are protected in the event of a mudslide. But soon they get preoccupied with other matters and continue to put off planning for the worst.

Fall comes and the rain doesn't stop. The ground below their property gets saturated and the area around their home begins to slide down the hill. The couple doesn't have an evacuation plan or insurance because they didn't plan ahead. So what happens when the ground begins to slip? They have an emergency on their hands. Like the inexperienced realtor described earlier, what could have been an inconvenience is now a crisis.

Scenarios like this happen everyday. An auto manufacturer gets on the front pages of the newspaper for vehicle accidents related to defective parts. The company hasn't planned to address this matter and now it finds itself at the center of negative publicity.

Thinking ahead and giving yourself realistic timelines will prepare you to deal with any last minute glitches. Usually the person who does not plan ahead is scrambling to get something done at the last minute. He is stressed out and unable to think clearly. And now an otherwise simple matter has become everyone's problem. But when you get organized, you will be able to set aside the time to plan and respond to most situations that arise. You will approach stressful circumstances with clarity and common sense. Remember, you'll be able to handle any urgent situation if you plan well.

The Pitfalls of Being Disorganized

No one sets out to begin a referral-based business with the intention of becoming miserably disorganized and buried under piles of paperwork. So why do so many people fail? It isn't because they lacked motivation or ability. After all, the desire to go out and do it says that these people are set apart from others. Failure happens because *they didn't make organization a priority*. Again, the system is simple. You just have to stay focused and understand that your success is all about staying organized.

Review

CRM's (Customer Relationship Management software, like Microsoft Outlook) are key to keeping track of your contacts, e-mails, and your client information. Learn to count on them like a trusted assistant. Remember, the software doesn't have to be the most expensive to be effective. Even free web-based e-mail can become a powerful business tool. The key is that you get into the habit of using your CRM all the time.

Using your CRM, setting realistic timelines, and planning for last minute glitches, will all give you peace-of-mind. The time you invest in getting and staying organized will reward you later. You will have time to resolve matters that could otherwise turn into emergencies and you'll work confidently, knowing that you are ready to meet your client's needs.

Chapter 4
Putting the Relationship Before the Paycheck

In the world of referral-based business, getting clients is the easy part. What's difficult is keeping them coming back. The healthy and consistent flow of work you're looking for comes from your ability to put relationships first, business second.

Why Does "Relationships First" Matter?

By putting relationships first, your friends and clients will immediately recognize that you are concerned about them and that you have their best interest at heart. On the other hand, when what comes across is how you will benefit from the relationship, most people will realize that your concern for them is insincere. You will make them less likely to trust you with their business or their friend's business.

This is especially important when you're starting out. Your initial business will most likely come from people you already know. And the personal service that you provide for those closest to you will ultimately translate into a referral.

For instance, let's say that Thomas is a loan officer just starting out on his own. During his training, he was taught what financial information he needed to gather from his clients and how to process the loan paperwork.

After a few months he has become a skilled officer. When he speaks with his clients he asks them to gather bank statements, paycheck stubs, and all other necessary paperwork. He collects the information from them, then begins the process of finding them a loan. While this level of service is fine for people who are working part time, this is not how you create and maintain a successful referral-based business.

The "relationships first" approach requires more effort and more interest in the well being of the client. For example, after years in the home loan business, Olivia learned that connecting with her clients on a personal level, getting to know them, and discovering their interests, were all just as important as gathering the correct information from them. What separates her from most of her colleagues is her relationships-first attitude of doing business.

Olivia takes the time to understand her clients' finances. She asks them to share their goals and concerns. In every transaction, she'll figure what her clients' long term plans are regarding their home purchase. She'll then gather the correct information from them and look for a loan that best meets their financial situation. Her objective is to give them the solutions they need to meet their goals.

After getting to know a particular client, Olivia will look over his finances. She may see that he has a car payment. She'll provide ways to help bring his car debt down by taking advantage of the many types of home loans available.

The Importance of Relationships

No matter what type of referral-based work you do, you have to understand the importance of relationships. It is through relationships that you will get business. After all, your commitment to your clients will help you understand how to meet their needs.

The real estate agent who only cares about the bottom line will try to close the deal as quickly as possible. Meanwhile, the one whose goal is to improve the lives of her clients looks carefully at what type of home will benefit her client's family most.

He customizes his services to best help his wide range of clients. He'll spend time with them and get to know them. This will give him the ability to discover what their interests are and what they're looking for—just like Olivia, the loan officer, who took time to understand the financial plans of her clients.

In one case, a client may want a larger house. She'll be willing to move farther from the city in order to get the house she is looking for. On the other hand, another person may enjoy the lifestyle of the city over the size of her home. This person will be more willing to live in a smaller house closer to the city.

The philosophy of putting your clients' needs first ultimately leads to your clients feeling comfortable with you. And in some cases (depending on your business) trusting you with their family's future.

Work With Who You Want To

Imagine your day filled with client meetings, where your clients are actually friends, and friends of friends. Think about how much you'll enjoy work when you're doing business with people that are already an important part of your life. Imagine how committed you'll be when you are serving people that are equally committed to you.

By the end of this chapter, you will have the tools to work with these types of people. The beauty of a referral-based business is that you can actually choose whom you want to work with. And let's be realistic, how many of your friends can say that about their jobs? But before you begin contacting friends and family, you need to have a well-organized contact list.

The 250 x 250 Rule

I have a challenge for you. Count how many people you know. Now, make that number grow to 250. How do you do this? Before I tell you, let's consider why this is important.

The 250 x 250 Rule goes like this: The 250 people you know each know 250 more people because it's not only who you know, but also who those people know. Initially, you may think that it is a daunting task to list 250 people. After spending some time doing this, you'll be surprised how many people you know. For instance, your friends, family, and almost everyone else in your phone book are most likely the first people you think of. But also consider old high school and college friends, your parent's friends, and colleagues from previous jobs.

Once you've listed 250 people, imagine this: If half of the people you knew gave you one new client you would have 125 clients per year of new business—more than enough work for one person to handle.

Initially, most people won't be able to write down 250 people they know. Regardless of how many people are on your list, it will range from those who are very close to you—people you contact regularly—to those you haven't contacted in months or years.

Next, gather and update the information you have about these people. Get out that address book where you have jotted down countless names, crossed out old addresses, and scribbled in new telephone numbers over old ones. Now, make this list as accurate and up-to-date as possible.

Take some time to go through your contact list and make all the information current. You are now ready to move on to the next step, which is organizing the people you know in the most effective way for your business.

Prioritize Your Contacts: Make a List of 1's, 2's, and 3's

Once the contact information for your friends and family is updated, you are ready to organize it simply and effectively.

The first part of grouping together your contacts is to decide which system you'll use. All of the relationships you have will fit into three categories. You can use 1's, 2's, and 3's; A's, B's, and C's; Platinum, Gold, and Silver, or whatever method you can remember best. In this book we will be using 1's, 2's, and 3's.

Your 1's are Your Biggest Supporters

At the top of the list are your 1's. These are the friends and family members closest to you: cousins, brothers, sisters, former colleagues, and anyone who has made a difference in your life. You trust your 1's and value your relationship with them more than anyone else. They are people you have known for years.

If you're starting out for the first time, your 1's are those that want to see you succeed and grow. They will refer business to you because they have your best interest at heart. Because these people are your biggest supporters, you should make the most effort to regularly contact them.

People like these are few and far between. In the beginning, you may have only a couple of people in this category. That's fine since your 1's are special individuals who can't easily be replaced. In all your relationships, you want to eventually bring as many people as you can into the 1's category.

Your Number 2's Are Potential 1's

Your 2's are close to you as well. The difference between 1's and 2's is that you are not their *only* source for referrals, although they refer business to you once in a while. You regularly see these people at social events, work, and through networking groups. Your 2's are people that are highly motivated to support you and in return you are trying to do the same for them. Most likely, you will have met many of these people through your 1's.

The good news is, once you've been introduced to your 2's through your 1's, you have a foundation to build a relationship from—because both of you share a common friend or colleague. That's because your 1's are important to you. Therefore, their friends and colleagues will most likely be people that you are eager to get to know as well. Make the effort to move 2's up to your 1 category.

Another difference between 1's and 2's is that you are still getting to know your 2's. You're still in the process of letting them know what you and your business are about. You most likely won't have a long history with them. On the other hand, both of you have the possibility of becoming strong business allies—that's why you put them in the 2's category.

Your 3's Are People that You Have Just Met

Your 3's are a transitional group. You are going to give yourself a couple of months to get to know them. In most cases, they are people that aren't going to give you referrals. As you get to know these people answer the following questions:

- Do we share similar work styles and will work well together?
- Is he or she worthy of my time and energy?
- Do I really want to do business with this person?

For instance, you're a financial planner and you've just met Ken. His sister happens to be a financial planner as well. Ken will most likely not refer business to you because of his relationship with his sister. On the other hand, he may end up being a trustworthy business colleague.

From him, maybe you can meet his sister and talk with her, get tips, and team up together. Keep in mind that being in the same business as someone else doesn't make them your adversary. You two may be focusing in different areas of business or different segments of the population. Make your colleagues your allies and your business will benefit.

Your 1's, 2's, and 3's must be people who are going to support your referral business. This means that a number 3 may never become a 2. A 3, however, can move into your personal address book and become a lifelong friend, rather than a business colleague.

Being Helpful: Becoming the "Go-To" Person

How many times have you heard people complain about how difficult it is to find good and reliable help? The truth is, once your business starts growing, you'll easily solve this problem for yourself, friends, family, and colleagues.

How? As you start to develop your contacts, you will start to create a strong group of people that make up your *referral team*—in other words, your list of primary contacts.

What is a referral team? A group of people that work under the highest standards of integrity and honesty—professionals just like you. And when friends and family ask you questions like, "Do you know a good CPA?" or "I need a good doctor, can you help me?" you will be prepared to connect them with the best people in their respective fields.

The benefit is two-fold: You support the businesses that you work with, and you gain respect and credibility from your biggest supporters—your 1's and 2's. Working with a referral team means that you become a better businessperson, friend, and community member. The following illustrates how a referral team works.

Steve Hallaway is a general contractor. He has had his own business for the last five years. Over the course of being a business owner, he has built a reputation for meeting his clients' needs. Although he's not the cheapest in town, he's definitely the most honest and dependable. This is in large part because of the way Hallaway Construction does business.

While building his business, Steve's referral team started

with plumbers, masons, and carpenters. Eventually, it grew to include dentists, hardware store owners, a florist, and almost any other business you can think of. Because his clients trusted him, they used the services he recommended to them even though they were completely unrelated to general contracting.

They felt confident that he knew the right people to get the project done. So when a client would share about her child's upcoming wedding, Steve was ready to suggest a great local florist. He would regularly hear back from the local businesses he supported—either through a simple thank you or a greeting card with a gift certificate enclosed.

But the biggest thank you came with a phone call that started with, "Hello Mr. Hallaway. My name is Rick and I was referred to you by Sandy, the owner of Floral Designs. I told her that I wanted to remodel my kitchen and she said that you could help me out."

Steve took these phone calls as the highest compliment. They were the ultimate reward for his style of doing business.

Just like Steve, when people think of you as a go-to person—someone who makes their lives easier—you gain credibility and respect. So next time you say, "Please let me know if I can help," be prepared to help your friend or family member out directly, or find the right person to take care of them the way you would.

Reviewing Your 1's, 2's, and 3's

Invest time to list 250 people you know, then update all the information you have for them. Next, organize them into three categories like 1's, 2's, and 3's.

Your 1's are those who are currently your biggest supporters. Often times these are your friends and family members. Your 2's are your potential 1's who refer business to you occasionally. You're still letting them know what you and your business are all about. Your 3's are people that you have just met. Because this is a transitional group, you're still determining whether or not they will be a good fit for your 1's or 2's categories.

You have to maintain an organized contact list in order to contact your clients in a systematic way. Together, this contact list and a philosophy that puts your clients' needs first, will allow you to grow and maintain a healthy referral-based business.

Chapter 5
Keeping in Touch

As you recall in Chapter 2: Getting Organized, you were given a list of five must-haves for your office:

1. A roomy, dedicated space
2. Files and file cabinet
3. Computer
4. Phone with voice mail
5. Combination printer/fax/copier/scanner

Followed by the five essentials to stay organized:

1. Document filing system
2. Banking system
3. To-do list
4. Calendar with personal appointments,
5. CRM (Customer Relationship Management software, like Microsoft Outlook)

You were guided, step-by-step, on how to get the most out of your CRM (Customer Relationship Management software such as Microsoft Outlook).

In Chapter 4 you learned how to organize your clients using the 1, 2, 3 system. Be certain you have updated your contact list and organized it in a three-part system before moving on to this section.

Now you are prepared to keep in touch with your clients, friends, family, and everyone else you network with.

Keeping in Touch Made Simple: A Sample Letter or e-mail to a Client

> Hi Lance and Kelly,
>
> I just wanted to say thank you for trusting me with your home remodel. It was really a pleasure to work with you. I hope that you enjoy your new kitchen.
>
> If you need anything feel free to contact me. I have a long list of quality businesses that I can refer you to.
>
> Your Friend,
> Nick
>
> P.S. I have included a couple of business cards that I hope you would give to people you know who could use my services.

Short, sweet, and personal. A message like this will go a long way to develop a relationship with your clients. By showing you have their best interest at heart you will generate repeat business. Because they trust you, you gain clients that you don't have to chase, but who will come to you when they need your service.

Networking Means *Socialize, Socialize, Socialize*

When you make the first contact you always want to be genuine. You also want to take the approach of listening more and talking less. People appreciate a person who takes time to listen to them.

For instance, let's say that you have met some people at a

networking event. First chat with them about their business. Next, get their cards and ask questions that will make them realize that you are interested in what they have to say.

Here are some questions you can ask them:

- How do they market themselves?
- How do they do business?
- What has worked for them and what hasn't?
- What do they enjoy most about what they do?
- How did they start out?
- What are the most valuable lessons they've learned?

Try your best to keep the conversation flowing. When they keep talking, it's a sign that they are comfortable with you. At first you will feel awkward, especially if you've never done this before. Eventually, however, holding a conversation will become a natural part of how you get to know people.

Make sure that you do not approach the conversation with a "here's why you need my business" mentality. The hard sell tactic will not win respect from those around you.

A better way is to think of the people you are speaking with as potential colleagues. You are talking with them to create business friendships. Enjoy yourself and have a good time. And if they need your service it is a bonus for you.

What to Do if You Get a Referral

As your reputation spreads throughout the community your list of contacts (1's, 2's, and 3's) will grow, which will ultimately lead to more referrals.

When a 1 gives you a phone number of a person she thinks you should contact, your life just got easier. When you contact this person for the first time, don't think of this as a cold call. After all, a colleague or friend has referred *their* colleague or friend to you. Now put yourself at ease—the connection you have with each other means that part of the relationship has already been established.

Here's how a general contractor would make the first call introducing himself to someone he was asked to contact. Modify this example to fit your needs:

"Hi, my name is Steve. A friend of ours, Karen, referred me to you. She told me that you may need some help with your home remodel.
"Karen spoke very highly of you and she told me that you're a great person.
"I'm more than willing to help a friend of Karen."

By beginning the conversation like this, you have personalized your message and created a connection. Next, you can talk about your relationship with Karen or anything that ties the three of you together. By talking about Karen you have moved your relationship many steps ahead of the traditional cold call. The conversation can now focus on the client's needs.

The One-Three Rule

One contact every three months will keep you at the forefront of your friends, family, and clients' minds. Follow this rule and the next time they need a home loan, real estate agent, or whatever service you provide, they'll contact you.

Imagine if you owned an auto body shop. Your friends,

family, or colleagues would not bring their cars to you unless they had a car accident or needed a paint job. The same is true for whatever you do. Your clients will not always need the service you provide everyday. So in the meantime, make sure that you keep in touch with them. When they do need your services, they'll let you know.

Another advantage of following the One-Three Rule comes when you are offering a new product or service. You will feel comfortable contacting your past clients, because it's not a cold call—it's a warm one. After all, you have consistently kept in touch with them once every three months.

Sticking with the One-Three Rule

Keeping in touch items for your 1's, 2's, and 3's include having on hand thank you cards, holiday cards, notes, and e-mails ready.

The best time to write a thank you or a holiday card is immediately after the transaction closes. Not months after when you don't remember why you are thanking them. Even if it's August and the temperature is 90 degrees outside write the Christmas card. (Hold it and send it out during the holiday.) You will need to do this to keep the message relevant. You will want to write the message when the relationship is still fresh in your mind.

You may feel that it will take too much time to write a personal message to all of your clients. If you prepare in advance, the process is easier than you think. Resist the temptation to use a word processor to print one letter and send it out to all your clients. The problem with this type of communication is it lacks the personal touch.

I recall a time when I visited a client. Sitting on her desk was the card I sent her. A local photographer created the thank you card I bought. Now every time my client sees the $5 beach scene on her desk, she'll think of my business. It definitely made the difference between a message that my client would keep, and one that would go straight into the trash. To learn how to keep in touch with your 1's, 2's, and 3's the easy way, follow the next five steps.

Five Simple Steps to Keep in Touch with Your Clients

Follow these steps and you will have a system in place that will guarantee that your 1's, 2's, and 3's are hearing from you once every three months.

1. Make a List
2. Purchase Cards that Reflect Your Personality
3. Soft Sell Your Message
4. Follow Up Once Every Three Months
5. Make a Contact Plan

1. Make a List

Go through your past and present clients. Make a list of all the people you would like to contact. (To find out more about this read Chapter 4: Putting the Relationship Before the Paycheck.)

2. Purchase Cards that Reflect Your Personality

Buy thank you cards, holiday cards, and note cards that show who you are. Make sure they stand out. This is an important step towards personalizing the message you give your clients. Don't skimp here. It may seem like a waste to spend money on expensive thank you cards, but the impression you leave will make it worth the investment. Form letters and pre-printed cards may be easier, but they are cold and impersonal. Handwritten letters are always best.

3. Soft Sell Your Message

Here's an example of a message I have sent to friends and family:

Hey Hannah and Miles,

I was just thinking about you guys today. I thought I would write you a card to say hi.

I've been pretty busy here with work and my family. I hope that your summer turned out great and all is going well.

Please call and tell me how you're doing. Maybe we can get together and get a cup of coffee soon.

Your Friend,
Cezar

P.S. Just in case you don't have my new contact info, I've included one of my cards.

Simple messages are best. They are easy for you to write and more importantly they are easy to read. They keep you at the forefront of your friends' and family's minds. Remember this: Go for the soft sell, not the hard one. Just tell them hi, you're thinking about them, and if they ever need your help, you're there.

Notice how the message to Hannah and Miles is friendly, *it's not selling a product or service.* In fact, it doesn't mention anything about what I do, or what I want from them. Instead, it's just letting my clients know that I am thinking about how they are doing.

This type of communication goes a long way to earning your clients' trust. They see how you are invested in the relationship and not just trying to get their business.

4. Follow Up Once Every Three Months

You've set the relationship up for success. You have organized how you'll contact the people most important to you and your business. You have also bought note cards that reflect your personality and you have written a warm message that doesn't directly ask for business.

At this point, follow up is easy. By sending them cards and e-mails, you have told them that you will be calling them soon without directly saying it. You have left the door open to contact them.

5. Make a Contact Plan

To consistently keep in touch with your present and past clients takes organization. After all, if you have a base of fifty clients, you will eventually find yourself swamped with letter writing. That is, if you don't organize how you are going to do it.

Successful realtors, financial planners, insurance agents, doctors, dentists, and all people that work by referral keep in contact with their clients in some systematic way.

If you decide to keep in touch whenever you have time,

you'll write 20 notes in one month and maybe four over the course of the next three. There are better ways to stay on top of this.

For example, if you have a large database of clients, plan to get in touch with them once every three months. If writing so many letters is overwhelming, write only a few letters at a time. Three or four a day, and you'll slowly chip away at the large list of clients you wish to contact.

If you are able to contact your clients once every three months, they'll receive something from you whether it's a phone call, e-mail, or written note, four times a year—a sure way to stay fresh in their minds. The goal is to maintain the relationship you have with your 1's, 2's, and 3's. As your business grows, this will become more difficult to do.

At times, you'll feel like the present clients you are working with are enough and you may neglect to contact past ones. Don't do this for long because once you've completed the projects for your present clients, you may find yourself without any new or repeat business. Keeping the work flow consistent (one of the hardest parts of being self-employed) means that you always have to meet your present clients' needs, while regularly keeping in touch with your past clients.

Now, the next section deals with what to do when you are busy with business today and at the same time, you find yourself unable to maintain contact with your past clients.

When Your Business Grows, Consider Hiring Extra Help

Follow-up is a simple process. Unfortunately, it takes time and needs to happen consistently. And as your client base grows, so will the demands of staying on top of business.

When business really gets busy, you may want to hire someone to help you. To start, ask a friend or family member for assistance, like a cousin or spouse.

For example, as your needs grow, you can hire someone a couple of hours per week. Consider the following: Pay someone $20 an hour, two hours per week, and have him or her label and get mailings out. For $160 per month, your return from repeat business will far exceed the amount you paid in getting someone to help you.

Review

In this chapter, you have learned the steps to stay in touch with your past and present clients. Remember, when meeting someone for the first time, listen more, talk less. Ask questions that will reflect genuine interest in the person you are speaking with.

Always go for the soft sell—show interest in creating connections and not in drumming up business. And stay in touch by following the five steps:

1. Make a List
2. Purchase Cards that Reflect Your Personality
3. Soft Sell Your Message
4. Follow Up Once Every Three Months
5. Make a Contact Plan

Finally, when you get too busy to stay in touch: First remember to celebrate—you're definitely making great progress; then consider hiring someone part-time to help you out. Remember, your referral-based business depends on your ability to keep your name fresh in the minds of friends, family, and past clients.

Chapter 6
Networking Means More Than Business Part 1: A New Approach to Getting Business

Scenario 1: Business Before Relationships

Chris was a talented and resourceful computer specialist. After working 10 years for a major software developer, he decided to follow his dream and open his own computer consulting business.

He spent months planning his big move. Within the last few weeks he purchased the retail space, the equipment, and had saved enough capital to get started. At this point he lacked only one thing—customers.

Before opening his business he spoke with some of his colleagues who have their own companies. He asked them about how to get started. One of them suggested that he join the local chamber of commerce.

Chris took this suggestion and paid the $250 membership fee. He received the new member packet. In it, he found a flier for an up coming business mixer.

The evening of the mixer he was both excited and nervous. He couldn't wait to get business. At the same time, working in a small department of another company meant that he had little networking experience. The thought of entering a room full of strangers, starting conversation, and asking for business made him anxious.

At 7:30 he walked into the chamber mixer. The environment was warm: People were shaking hands, passing out business cards, and talking in small groups. As he walked around, Chris could feel his pulse speeding up. The slight twitch in his hand told him he was uncomfortable. He had never attended a function like this before. He finally gathered the courage to enter a conversation.

Chris introduced himself to the circle of people he approached. He shook their hands and they all exchanged business cards.

Later on in the evening when announcements were made, he was recognized as a new member. He received a plaque and warm applause from his fellow chamber members. "These are friendly people, I'm glad I attended," he told himself.

Towards the end of the event, he spoke to a small business owner. Marco was looking to upgrade his current computer system. This was exactly the type of business Chris was looking for. They exchanged business cards and Marco promised to meet Chris at his store the next day to discuss how to proceed.

Chris left the chamber meeting excited. Over the course of two hours, he passed out several business cards, told people about his business, and even received a solid lead. The advice he received from his colleague paid off—joining the chamber of commerce was a solid way to meet people…so he thought.

The next day came. No phone calls and Marco didn't come by. Disappointed, but still motivated, Chris continued to attend chamber mixers. After two months of diligently attending meetings, passing out business cards, and honing his networking skills, no business came.

He decided that the chamber was not the best avenue for him. After all, he had done exactly what his colleagues had told him to do and he still had no new clients. Frustrated and disillusioned, not to mention his bills piling up, Chris was uncertain about the future of his new company.

Scenario 2: Relationships First

Tony is a CPA who, up to this point, has worked for a prominent downtown accounting office. Upon the advice and encouragement of his friends and family, he has decided to start his own firm.

Like Chris, he meets with local small business owners to get some advice. The owner of a financial planning firm in town tells him that the local chamber of commerce is a great way to create business.

But before joining, he has coffee with a colleague that he worked with a couple of years ago. Tiffany was one of the top-performing CPA's in the downtown office before she decided to open her own firm.

Tony phones Tiffany and invites her to coffee. The two worked closely together at the CPA firm and she was more than happy to meet with her old friend.

They arrange to meet at Cup o' Java, a coffee house close to her office.

"Tiffany, it's great to see you again. How long has it been since we last saw each other?"

"Too long. Gosh, I think it was when you all took me out to lunch my last day at the firm. Remember that?"

"That's right. Has it been that long? That must've been at least two years ago."

"Almost three, I remember because I officially started my business the next week."

"How's that going?"

"It's great. The first year or so it was pretty rough. But now, I'm finally getting the hang of this whole self-employment thing."

"You're a pretty remarkable person," he says.

"Not really. But I am a hard worker. Speaking of self-employment when are *you* going out on your own?" she laughs as she says this.

"Actually, as crazy as this sounds, I'm starting my own firm too."

"Great news! You've got the talent, that's for sure. What made you want to?" she asks.

"I'd been talking to some friends, I know some pretty entrepreneurial types, you know, self-starters. They've been telling me for years that I'm crazy working for someone else."

"They're right. But wanting is one thing. Actually doing is a whole 'nother. It's definitely not for the light hearted," she says.

"I know. That's what has kept me at the office. It seemed like such a big move to quit and start out on my own."

"Yeah, it definitely takes a certain type of person. But now that my business is moving forward, I wouldn't ever want to go back," she says.

"Well, Tiffany, you probably figured this out by now. That's one reason I wanted to meet. Now that I'm starting my own business, I wanted to get some advice from you."

"Hey, any chance to help out a friend," she says.

"Thanks. It means a lot to me," he says.

"Listen, what goes around, comes around. Like I said, these past couple of years have been pretty rough. Thank goodness that I've had some amazing people come through for me. I'm excited that I can actually help someone else now."

"Well I'm ready to listen to whatever you have to say. Here's my question. I have friends who've told me to join the chamber of commerce where I live. What do you think?"

"That's a great idea. It worked for me in the beginning…of course, if you wanted to join *my* chamber, I would tell you it's a terrible idea," she laughs, knowing that Tony planned to join a chamber in another city.

"But there are some key steps you have to take to establish your name in the chamber." Tiffany takes a sip of coffee and continues, "If you don't, you'll be wasting your time passing out business cards that'll go right in the trash."

"Like what kind of steps? It seems pretty straightforward. Become a member, go to a couple of mixers, and over time get to know people," he says.

"You can try that. But trust me, you'll never get your name out that way…and in a few months you'll be frustrated, give up, and want to try something else."

"What do you mean?" he asks.

"You have to make a name for yourself. Otherwise, you're just another badge wearing member. No one special, no one anyone will remember."

"Make a name for myself. That makes sense," he says.

"It does, doesn't it? You have to become more than a member. You've got to become an *active participant* by establishing your credibility with key members."

"But doesn't that take time? After all, they don't know me yet. Isn't that something to aim for after a few months?"

"Yes, for most people it takes months and even years. That's because most of them don't have any idea how to become a chamber member the right way. Don't get me wrong, their hearts are in the right place—they want business. They just don't know any better. And they end up wasting a lot of time networking in a way that doesn't help them get where they want to go."

"Now you've got me hooked. How do I join the *right way*?" he asks.

Tiffany puts her mug down. She leans towards Tony and speaks in a hushed tone.

"Here's the secret to earning the respect and trust of key members in the chamber or any other networking group you join. Do what I tell you and you'll save months and even years. You'll become an important player in no time," she says.

In three simple steps, Tiffany explains to Tony what he needs to do.

Tony's First Chamber Mixer

Tony shows up at the restaurant that just opened its doors two weeks ago.

He is excited to put the advice Tiffany gave him to use. He enters the restaurant, gets a drink, and walks around. Tony carefully looks at the nametags of people in the crowd. He notes the members who are part of chamber committees.

He sees four people in the room who have tags that read, "Carla Barksdale: Women's Council Committee Member," "Larry Ineno: President's Circle Committee Member," "Barbara Doyle: Technology Committee Member," and "Albert Dominguez: Special Events Committee Member."

He remembers Tiffany's first tip, Step 1:
Get Involved—Right Away.

She told him it was critical that he met people actively involved in the chamber, not people who simply attended mixers.

Tony recalls Tiffany saying that the fastest way to find the most active members is through committee work. He considers what committee he would like to join. The finance committee seems right down his area of expertise…but he thinks that every other CPA in the chamber probably has the same thoughts.

He has always had an interest in computers. So he decides to speak with Barbara Doyle, Technology Committee member.

When he approaches her, she is speaking with three other people. She is engaged in conversation, and by looking at how the two next to her are hanging on her every word, she obviously commands respect. Tony enters the conversation and introduces himself.

"Hi my name is Tony Abdulah," he glances at Barbara's nametag and says, "I see that you're part of the Technology Committee."

"I sure am. Are you into computers?" she asks.

"Actually, I'm a CPA, but technology is something that I've always been interested in. I just became a member of the chamber a few days ago."

"Welcome to the club. You'll definitely find it worthwhile. How's it been so far? We haven't scared you away yet have we?" she says with a smile on her face.

Tony is put at ease with her sense of humor. "It's been great, thank you. I was wondering, does your committee meet regularly and is it open to all members?"

"Yes, as I was telling Adela and Rick here, we meet once a month. And the meetings are open to all members."

Tony asks for Barbara's business card, as well as Rick's and Adela's. He hands them his in return. He asks them to give him a call if they know of any other networking groups that he might be interested in.

The following Tuesday, Tony shows up at the Technology Committee meeting. Barbara introduces him to the 10 other committee members. Everyone exchanges business cards. He sits in the meeting and enjoys the discussion about how the group plans to improve the chamber's Web site.

At this moment, he remembers the next tip that Tiffany told him, Step Two: ***Give and You Will Receive.***

The committee determines that the chamber needs a new Web site. They decide to form a sub-committee to find the best web developers based on available funds. Tony offers to join the sub-committee. He recently updated his Web site and was pleased with the person that did his web design. He realizes that this is the perfect opportunity to share this information with his new colleagues.

After a couple subcommittee meetings, he gets to know two members. He feels comfortable enough to ask them if they would like to meet for coffee later during the week.

Next, he puts Tiffany's final step to work, Step Three: ***Focus on the Relationship, Not the Business.***

He meets with one committee member over coffee, Tony asks Travis about his family and what he likes to do for fun. All of his questions reflect a genuine interest his new friend's life.

The conversation turns to Tony. Travis asks him what he does for a living. Although he is embarrassed, Tony is honest and tells him that he's just starting his own business. Travis shares his experience with him about going out on his own and gives him some worthwhile advice.

He continues to develop relationships within the committee. In a matter of weeks he earns the trust of key members in the chamber.

Three committee, two subcommittee meetings, and one cup of coffee later, a chamber member refers a friend to Tony. The client was easy to work with and was very pleased with Tony's work.

Tony continues to build relationships with his colleagues in the chamber, and they begin referring more and more business to him. The process didn't happen overnight. But slowly he's building a reputation for excellent work.

He has avoided the cold calls, the mailings, and the print ads that many of his colleagues invest time and money in. And the best part is, he is working with people who are pleasant, treat him well, and refer business to him.

Review

What Went Wrong with Chris? And What Went Right with Tony?

Chris, the computer business owner, took some important steps before branching out on his own. He spoke with small business owners and took their advice. Unfortunately, once he joined the chamber, he didn't get to know anyone. He simply handed out his business cards, and didn't attempt to build connections with people—he was putting business over relationships.

On the other hand, Tony put his priority on relationships. He realized that when it came to starting a referral-based business, building relationships was essential.

The key difference between the two approaches is this: Tony gave his time to the chamber technology committee. In turn, he received a referral from a committee member.

As for Chris, he was *only* focused on receiving; he was preoccupied with drumming up business and overlooked the relationships that he needed to build first.

When you set out to create lasting relationships for your business follow these steps:

Step 1: Get Involved—Right Away

If you decide to join a networking group (like a local chamber of commerce) find out who you need to contact. Then join a committee to get to know key members of the group.

Step 2: Give and You Will Receive

Once you have gotten to know people within the networking group, see what you can contribute. Is there a service or skill that you can offer? Or is there an event that you can volunteer to help plan? Find out how you can give and you will see the benefits.

Step 3: Focus on the Relationship, Not the Business

Once you get to know certain people within the group, ask

them to meet over coffee. Coffee is easy since it can last a short time or a long time depending on how you connect.

Show genuine interest and ask about their business. Remember, talk less, listen more. For more tips on how to network with others and get to know them better, read Chapter 5: Keeping in Touch.

In life, the more time you help people and the more you get involved, the more you will receive. Manage your business the same way and be ready to embrace what's out there for you.

Chapter 7 Networking Means More Than Business Part 2: Three Words To Live By

In three simple words here's how you network: *Socialize, Socialize, Socialize.*

What is Networking?

When you think about the word networking, imagine the Internet. It's basically a large computer system; the computers, telephones, and electrical systems are all connected through wires. And when you narrow it down, one wire connects all these systems together. Your business is the same. You are one part of a network connected to tens, hundreds, and even thousands of other people.

Tap into this vast pool of people and your success is inevitable. But to do this you have to push yourself. You need to meet people who will connect you with their friends and colleagues.

Tell People What You Do

Before I explain how you do this, let me describe what not to do.

DO NOT TRY TO SELL YOURSELF. Throughout life you have come across people who only talk about what they do for a living. Their lives revolve around business and what they can get from you. People on the extreme end of this only show interest in those who will move them ahead. If you are setting out to create a successful referral-based business, becoming like one of these people is the fastest way to alienate your friends and colleagues.

Now how do you avoid the hard sell? Keep in mind, you're not selling yourself, you're just meeting people and letting them know what you do. The key here is to socialize with people—who like you—put others first.

Five Ways to Network

Effective networking requires you to become creative. Think about the activities you do on a regular basis and who you see everyday. Here are five examples of how you can integrate networking into daily life:

1. Volunteer in Your Community/ Place of Worship
2. Join a Homeowner's Association
3. Volunteer at School
4. Play a Team Sport or Become a Soccer Mom or Dad
5. Join a Networking Group

1. Volunteer in Your Community/ Place of Worship

The key word here is *volunteer.* For instance, by simply attending your place of worship and leaving, you'll never meet anyone. You've got to volunteer. There are several ways that you can do this. If you have a faith-based tradition and meet regularly with people who share your similar beliefs, networking opportunities are waiting for you.

Become active in your church, synagogue, mosque, temple,

or other place of worship. When you get involved, you are connecting yourself with outstanding members of the community who also share your values.

You can make great friends and contacts here—people who have the potential to become your number 1's. For instance, you can attend a study group, help organize events, or join a committee. Working side-by-side with people like yourself will allow you to socialize and meet possible clients. At the same time, your service will benefit the community.

2. Join a Homeowner's Association

If you live in a housing development that has an HOA (Homeowner's Association) try running for a position on the board. By running for office two things happen: People in the community get to know who you are; and you will work closely with fellow board members. If you are elected, you'll have the opportunity to network with board members and other homeowners through monthly meetings and social gatherings. Thus you'll expose yourself to potential new clients and expand your referral base.

3. Volunteer at School

This is the perfect way to network if you have children. You can volunteer at your child's school a few hours a week, become an active member of your PTA, or both. In either case, you'll be making a difference in your child's life.

Just like the HOA or place of worship, you'll expose yourself to new clients and expand your referral base. While you're making contacts, you'll spend valuable time with your kids and other parents, you'll get to know your children's friends, and you'll meet their teachers.

4. Play a Team Sport or Become a Soccer Mom or Dad

Sports fans, this one is for you. Become a coach or get on a sports team. Either participate on a team, or you can offer to coach a children's team. Soccer, softball, basketball, you name it, these sports are always looking for parents to help out by coaching or planning events. The idea is the same—put yourself in a position to meet other people and socialize, while in the process enjoying yourself.

5. Join a Networking Group

The local chamber of commerce or networking groups are great sources for referrals. Take this approach and your business will be better for it: Join the group to meet people *after* the meetings.

Once you get to know a couple of people within the group, begin asking them if they would join you for coffee. Coffee is great because you both have an out. It can be a meeting for 10 minutes, or one that lasts two hours. During this time you will get to know each other. Meet with them one-on-one and you'll learn about their interests and the type of personality they have. For more tips on this, read Chapter 6: Networking Means More Than Business Part 1.

I hope that by reading the last five tips, you get the idea: With the exception of the last one, networking means more than just business settings or attending events called "Networking Meetings." The interactions you have everyday are perfect opportunities to share about what you do.

For instance, let's say you have children. When you take them to the park or another public place, who else is around you? (Answer: other parents). Chat with them. After you get to know them set up a play date. If they are from another country, ask: "Did you grow up here, or somewhere else?" or "How long have you lived in this area?" You will be surprised at the amount of information people are willing to share when they feel comfortable around you.

The list certainly extends beyond the five tips that I just gave you. Get creative and see how you can turn everyday social interactions at the gym, daycare, or wherever, into networking opportunities. For more information about networking groups, log onto www.biznetclub.com.

What to Say, What to Ask

I just stated that people are willing to share a great deal of information about their lives if they feel comfortable around you. How do you create this environment of comfort without medieval spells and truth serums? Ask the right questions.

We are social beings. People are open to share about their lives if they trust you. If you are sincere and communicate clearly, those around you will notice. Still not convinced? How about in your life? You are probably able to spot a reckless, in-your-face, salesperson a mile away…well, so can others.

Like you've read earlier, getting business is the easy part. But developing a network of family and friends takes time and effort. You can do this by showing interest in them first and talking about your business *only* when it's appropriate. When you approach it this way, people will always feel comfortable talking with you about your business.

When you are meeting people at a place that indicates something about their lives, a long list of questions can emerge. Let's say you're meeting them at an elementary school. You can ask a series of questions regarding their child: How do they like their school? What do they like about their child's current teacher? The list goes on.

Networking Can Happen When You Least Expect It

This next scenario points out how networking can be a part of your daily life.

Rick and his wife Julie arrive at a friend's wedding reception. As they approach the table Rick sees the names of the guests who will sit next to them.

He smiles when he recognizes the names Ken and Kathleen Davis on the name cards that sit above the fancy dinner setting. Ken and Kathleen are friends that he and Julie haven't seen for years.

"Hey, Julie. Guess who's sitting with us tonight?" he says.

"Who?" she asks.

"Ken and Kathleen Davis. Remember how we used to go on movie dates together?"

"That's right. Those were fun times, back when we actually had time to do that kind of stuff. I can't wait to see them."

He and his wife sit down. When Ken and Kathleen arrive at the table, all four or them exchange warm hugs and handshakes.

Julie realizes that she and Rick have left the wedding present in their car. She tells her husband, then excuses herself from the table to get it. Rick starts catching up with his friends.

"So, what are you guys up to these days?" he asks.

"Gosh, our lives have changed so much since Tommy was born," says Kathleen.

"You can say that again," adds Ken.

"How old is he now?" Rick asks.

"Tommy's already three," she says.

"Wow, three years old. Kathleen, are you still working? I mean, at a job outside of your home since I know that being a mom is tough work."

"It sure is hard work. I never imagined how much it would take to raise a child. I'm really grateful that Ken has a job that can support us."

"You are lucky. My wife and I are doing the same thing," says Rick.

"That's right, your daughter. How old is Payton now?" asks Ken.

"Can you believe it? She's already five."

"Time definitely goes fast once you start having kids. Hey, what are you doing for work these days?" asks Ken.

"Well, my business is going well. We just moved offices a couple of months ago."

"I'm sorry. It's been so long. What kind of business do you do again?" asks Ken.

"I'm a mortgage broker."

"Now I remember. Listen, we've got to talk…What do you think? Is it a good time to refinance now? Kathleen and I have been thinking about it."

"Yeah. It's a great time. But before we talk business, tell me more about Tommy. Where is he now? Julie and I would love to meet him."

Julie returns with the present. She sits down.

"Hey Julie, did you know that Ken and Kathleen have a three year old son?"

"Congratulations, that's fantastic," she says.

All four of them have a lively conversation. After the reception they exchange numbers and decide to go out for a movie later that month.

Put the Relationship Above the Paycheck

When Rick heard Ken's interest in refinancing his home, notice how Rick didn't insist on talking about work. You may think that he missed an opportunity to generate business, but his approach to networking puts the relationship first, not business.

Is Rick going to get business that night? Probably not. But that wasn't his goal when he and his wife showed up at the reception. On the other hand, when Ken and Kathleen need someone to refinance their loan, who will they ask? And when they have a friend who needs a home loan, whose business card will they give them? The answer is clear. By putting the relationship first, Rick has reconnected with old friends and expanded his client base at the same time.

Follow-up is key to making moments like the wedding scenario just described successful. After the initial contact, the phone call, thank you note, or e-mail must happen right away.

Think about it this way. In families there is always someone who keeps members together. If it weren't for this person, many family get-togethers wouldn't happen, information about brothers, sisters, aunts, and uncles wouldn't be shared, and communication would be less efficient. In your business, you need to be that person. When you do this, you'll see results.

Review

Socialize, Socialize, Socialize

If it were up to me, I'd like to get rid of the word networking and change it to *socializing*. That is what skilled referral-based business people do. They listen, they ask questions, and they show genuine interest in the people that they are speaking with.

Remember the five ways you can make networking a part of daily life:

1. Volunteer in Your Community/ Place of Worship
2. Join a Homeowner's Association
3. Volunteer at School

4. Play a Team Sport or Become a Soccer Mom or Dad
5. Join a Networking Group

Networking is more than a skill, it's learned thinking. With practice you'll become better at it. You'll think of new ways to seize opportunities to talk to others and show interest in their lives. After all, the more you put into a relationship, the more comes back to you. So remember, *Socialize, Socialize, Socialize.* Get involved, give of yourself, and get ready to receive.

Chapter 8
Working With Difficult Clients

We've all had them. Most of the time their comments are subtle. They ask you the same question over and over again. They tell you things like, "I read about a better offer the other day," or "I heard that I can get a cheaper price by doing this..." They call you frequently.

Once in a while you'll get the direct hit. A person might say something like, "I'm not sure you're getting me the best deal." Fortunately this rarely happens.

All of these examples point to one thing. Whether your clients say it explicitly or not, they are feeling uncomfortable and are afraid that you (or they) are making the wrong decision. These people are what I call "stress creators"—regardless of how good a situation is, they will always feel some type of anxiety about it…and they will want you to feel the same way.

In a perfect world, your clients will know that you're the expert. They will listen to your suggestions and will follow through with your advice. They will ask you important questions and trust you to answer them. But we work in the real world—one where people have doubts and anxiety. They need to let out their frustration. And at some point in your career they will let it out on you.

Know Who You're Working With

After meeting with a few clients and getting some experience behind you, you'll soon know how to read a client. As you work with more and more people you'll quickly determine who will be relaxed and who will be difficult.

For instance, you may notice that a client asks a lot of questions. All conscientious people should ask questions, and you should listen to their concerns. But I'm referring to concerns that question your ability to provide them what they're looking for.

Learning to Let Go

The following point is difficult to swallow: *Be willing to let clients go if they fail to trust you.* I realize that when you're starting out, you'll be reluctant to turn anyone away. Your concern is understandable. And at the beginning you may have to work with difficult people in order to keep your business afloat. But be warned, DON'T DO THIS FOR LONG.

As soon as you have established a comfortable group of clients, be selective about who you want to work with. Don't work with people who will put your hard work and integrity into question. Otherwise, you'll always have clients who will make you question your ability to provide quality service.

Why Letting Go is Good Business

When deciding whether a client should go elsewhere to get the service he needs, you may think that this is exactly what you should not do. You may say to yourself, "No customer is perfect and I have to be flexible and stick things out."

On the other hand, consider all the time and energy you

commit to these people. Are they worth the late evening and weekend phone calls? Do you need the stress that keeps you up at night? What about the feeling that you aren't being trusted? In some cases, because you want to please them and give them a good experience, you will make compromises.

For instance, let's say that you're a cabinetmaker. You've been making and installing cabinets for years. While humble, you're confident about your ability to provide quality craftsmanship and service.

But your client is not easy to deal with. As you work with him, he will change the materials that he originally asked for, as well as the plans. All of which will ultimately delay the completion date. When that date rolls around, he'll blame you for missing it. Meanwhile, he continues to question your fees and your craftsmanship.

Because of your high standards, you will initially doubt your abilities. You may even question the type of service and craftsmanship you provide, despite knowing that you did an excellent job. Perhaps to make him happy you'll think about reducing your fees. Even though you know that he's already getting a good deal.

Instead, you could have left this client behind. In the time that you wasted dealing with his unreasonable demands, you could have been networking, drumming up more business, and getting organized.

What to Say to a Difficult Client

When you realize that a client is creating more work for you than is necessary and hassles you over petty matters, say something like this:

"I sense that you don't completely trust me in this situation. Perhaps it would be better if you worked with someone you trusted. If you like, I have someone who I can refer you to."

When you tell clients this, remember that they don't really know you and they don't know if they can trust you. *So you must tell them in a professional and sincere manner.* Saying this to them forces them to think about what they want: Do they really want to start the whole process over again with someone else?

Keep in mind that you must mean what you say. You must be willing to let them go. You have to believe that you have done your best and tried your hardest. Remember, people are referring business to you because you're doing good work. And after all you've done, if someone is unwilling to trust you, then it's best for both of you that he or she looks elsewhere.

The good news is that after you tell your clients this, most will stay with you. They will realize that you have their best interest at heart. They may even deny that they ever mistrusted you.

Sometimes Working With Difficult Clients Can Be Good For You

After working with several difficult clients your communication skills will improve. You'll also notice that someone who would have been a difficult client before, is easier to work with now. This is because you will have developed the skills to know what to say and how to make them feel at ease.

When you have dealt with tens and hundreds of clients, you

will be able to manage almost any situation. You will know how to make a stressed and anxious client feel reassured and relaxed. You may even look forward to a difficult client as a challenge—a test of your ability to communicate well.

The Secret to Earning Your Client's Trust: Manage Their Expectations

The way you earn your clients' trust is through repeated actions that give them peace of mind. There are two ways to do this:

1. Manage their expectations.
2. Let them know how you do business.

1. Manage Expectations

Many people have a fear of missing deadlines. This makes sense. More often than not, something like this occurs:

Imagine you sub-contract a job out for a client. The sub-contractor quotes you two to three days to complete the project. You tell those dates to your client, but it ends up taking four or five days instead. Now you'll have some explaining to do—even though you weren't the one responsible for the delay.

Remember that timelines are key to establishing your credibility. Unfortunately, many people establish timelines that don't give them any room for error or unplanned circumstances.

Here's a simple solution that will not only give your clients the dates and times that will reassure them, but will protect yourself as well: Pad your time or give yourself buffers, such as adding an extra day or two in a quote.

If you believe that a project will take five days to complete, make it eight instead. This way you will always be on time or even early. After all, you must be prepared to handle any urgent situation that will come up. All the planning in the world won't keep you from running into difficulties. When your deadline doesn't give you room for last minute glitches, you'll miss your target date.

Thus determine your deadlines wisely and set your clients up to expect the best from you. Then you'll never be caught in a situation where you're left with no room for error, even if it was someone else's mistake that has put you in this awkward position.

Keep in mind most people hear what they want to. If you tell them a project will be completed in three or four days, they'll hold you responsible for the three, not the four. I'll go in depth about how to determine your deadlines in Chapter 9: Managing Expectations and Working Through Difficult Situations.

2. Let Them Know Your Business Hours

You've now padded your time to give you room to deal with last minute glitches and mange your clients' expectations. Next, tell them your business hours. That way they'll know when they can reach you.

For instance, let all your clients know that your business hours are from 9:00 a.m. to 5:00 p.m. Then tell them to call you anytime during those hours. Also, let them know that if they contact you after hours, you'll return their call the next business day. Now when you return their call at 6 PM—an hour after you're closed—they are impressed because you made an extra effort to contact them.

Review

Know Who You're Working With

Some easy ways to determine whether a client is truly difficult or just needs your reassurance, is to ask yourself:

- Have I done everything I could to communicate with them?
- Are they being unreasonable?
- Do I need to let this person go?

Learning to Let Go

If dealing with your client isn't worth the stress, the time spent addressing endless demands, and the anxiety that keeps you up at night, let them go.

Why Letting Go is Good Business

The time that you waste dealing with the unrcasonable demands of a difficult client can be better spent networking, drumming up more business, and getting organized.

What to Say to a Difficult Client

In your business you realize that trust between you and your clients is essential. When they question your ability to do quality work, be ready to sincerely and politely let them go. You can start off by saying something like:

"I sense that you don't completely trust me over this situation. Perhaps it would be better if you work with someone you trust. If you like, I have someone who I can refer you to."

Sometimes Working With Difficult Clients Can Be Good For You

After you have dealt with tens and hundreds of clients, you will be able to manage almost any situation and help them feel at ease with the process. By including people who many would consider "difficult clients" you will increase your client base.

The Secret to Earning Your Client's Trust: Manage Their Expectations

The way you earn your client's trust is through repeated actions that give them peace-of-mind. There are two ways to do this:

1. Manage their expectations.
2. Let them know how you do business.

The key to avoiding awkward situations is to manage your clients' expectations. Give them clear timelines with enough padding—you never know what problem may arise in your project. Finally, let your clients know your business hours; then surprise them by providing service that goes beyond their expectations.

Chapter 9
Managing Expectations and Working Through Difficult Situations

Take it from project managers who work for the world's largest corporations. They handle multi-million dollar accounts and deal with multiple vendors and hundreds, if not thousands of people. They realize that innumerable factors are out of their control. Therefore, they put extra time into planning to make sure that everything is under control and completed when promised.

When you learn to give yourself enough time to get the job done right you avoid crises and complications. By setting realistic timelines, you can still meet your deadlines, despite any urgent situation that comes up. You have enough time to take care of matters that would make others stressed and anxious. Why?

While the other guy is scrambling to get everything together, perhaps running behind schedule and waiting for someone else to come through, you sit back and relax. The extra time you put into planning—like setting up buffers for your deadlines—has put you in a place where you have things under control. You are calm and enjoy the process.

Think of Yourself as a Project Manager

Imagine that you're a project manager for Toyota or IBM. Your business may not be as big as the corporations that these project managers work for. But there is a lot to learn from them that will make your business better than anyone else's.

Regardless of how small your company is, you have the same responsibilities and pressures as a project manager who works for a major corporation. You are in charge of making things happen on time. You determine when a job gets done. Meanwhile, your clients, supervisor, or both, are counting on you to stick to your deadlines.

Drawing from Your Resources

Missing or meeting deadlines reflect your performance. That's exactly why you will choose people who will get the job done right.

Refer to your number 1's. They are people that you will count on throughout your career. You know how they do business, you know exactly what to expect from them, and you know they get things done on time.

Your 1's are just as committed to making sure the job gets completed as you are. Your project is their project. Number 1's are your friends *and* colleagues. Your commitment to each other drives both of you to do your best.

As you've experienced throughout your life, your friends do extra for you. They work harder, they stay late to meet deadlines, and they'll do whatever it takes to finish a task. And you will do the same for them.

Keep in mind that you need to remain flexible. For instance, let's say that someone you work closely with doesn't always stick to deadlines, *but* he provides excellent service. If you want to continue to work with him, you'll have to pad the timeline of your project.

With this group of reliable, dependable people lined up, your business is ready to take on almost anything.

What To Do When Things Go Wrong

Unfortunately, no matter how hard you plan ahead, work with the right people, and stay on your timeline, once in awhile you will make a mistake.

For instance, you are a contractor. You're installing new flooring. You realize that you miscalculated the square footage and you don't have enough to cover the floor. Now you have to spend more money, or should I say more of your client's money, and you have to tell her this *today.*

When this happens don't call your client to simply tell her the problem. Call her with a solution as well.

Here are three things to do to help you save face:

1. Stop and Think
2. Ask for Help
3. Call Your Client

1. Stop and Think

Before calling your client, take time and think the matter through. Do this regardless of how pressing or urgent the situation is. This is key to finding out how you're going to fix the problem. Ask yourself, "What is the best solution and how do I communicate it?"

2. Ask for Help

Call some colleagues or friends whom you trust. You need someone to consider your ideas. Tell them what happened and listen to their suggestions. You have a problem on your hands and you need to talk to those you respect in order to find a solution. Once you've figured out what to do, then…

3. Call Your Client

You've gone through step one and two. You are now in control and have clear direction. At this point, you are ready to solve the problem. Even though the direction you are headed isn't as beneficial to the client as planned, you have a solution that will meet her needs.

Your goal is to make her feel secure knowing that you have her best interest at heart. After all, you know that you have done everything possible to improve the situation. By following these three steps you are putting yourself in a place that tells the client you have everything under control. You are speaking to her with clear plans and you are prepared to address her concerns.

Now, you're prepared to take the next step, which is the most important.

Post-Game Analysis

Once you have dealt with the issue directly, you must reflect on what happened. Review the entire process and recall the events that lead up to the problem. For example, if you missed a deadline because of a holiday weekend, add it into the timeline you will use next time.

In the case of the contractor who miscalculated the amount of flooring he needed for the home, before bidding for the next project, he needs to go over what caused him to make the mistake in the first place. He will need to put a system in place that is easy to use and will ensure that he will not make the same mistake again.

This may sound simple—and it is. But how many people do you know who thoroughly evaluate a problem situation? The key is to take the guesswork out of what went wrong. Otherwise, you will repeat the mistake again. Analyzing and solving the root cause of the problem is critical to reducing the risk of error.

In the corporate world, this process of review is called Practical Problem Solving. You set systems in place. You understand how they work. What works well stays; what doesn't changes.

Practical Problem Solving constantly reduces error and improves the quality of your product or service. The key is to learn from your mistakes and the mistakes of others. When you approach work from the perspective of a project manager, you'll become more efficient at what you do. Take the time to review your process. All the while, think of ways to minimize risks and mistakes.

Review

Think of Yourself as a Project Manager

Remember that regardless of the size of your business you have the same responsibilities as a project manager who works for a large company. You are in charge of making things happen on time.

Drawing from Your Resources

When you work with your 1's, friends, and colleagues, you know that they are just as committed to getting the job done as you are. Your project is their project.

What To Do When Things Go Wrong

1. Stop and Think
2. Ask for Help
3. Call Your Client

Post-Game Analysis

You will need to put a system in place that is easy to use and will ensure that you will not make the same mistake again. The key is to take the guesswork out of what went wrong. Otherwise, you will repeat the mistake again. Analyzing and solving the root cause of the problem is critical to reducing risk of error.

Chapter 10
Remain Focused: Stay True to Your Goals

Starting and developing a referral-based business doesn't happen overnight. It will take time. Give yourself at least a year or two of hard work.

During these first years, you may have evenings like this:

It's late at night. You can't sleep. The stress runs so strong you can almost touch it. Thoughts spin around your head because you don't know what to do. You know that the reason for your anxiety is that you've got bills to pay and no money to cover them.

All of us who have a full time referral-based business have been there at least once. Many of us have had countless nights like these. The pressure and the feeling of despair are enormous. You are consumed with thoughts of doubt: Is this for me? Am I making the right choices? Do I need to look for other work?

The anxiety makes sense. Let's say your bills are $3,000 per month. If you don't have cash reserves and six months pass you would have $18,000 of debt. That would be enough to cause stress for any small business owner.

View these lean times as a test of your will. You are being pushed to your limits. You are questioning who you are and what you believe in. Will you have the tenacity and the desire to stay the course? Or are you going to cave under the pressure? This is precisely the time, when doubt runs high, that you see what you are made of.

Stand firm in your commitment to accomplish what you set out to do. After all, you have planned, done the research, and know that others have successfully accomplished what you are setting out to do. Success is often just around the corner.

Success Stories Come Through Failure

If you are feeling like a complete failure, you need to understand that in order to accomplish a major goal you often have to fail. Remember, success is no accident. It is the result of the determination to meet your goals. Anyone who thinks that success comes purely from good luck doesn't really know what success is.

You must decide whether you are going to ultimately reach your goals and then you must push forward with everything you have. Instead of thinking, "I don't have what it takes to succeed." You must think, "I'll do whatever I need to make it happen."

Think of all the people who have overcome the most difficult circumstances and reached their goals. Many of them accomplished what they set out to do, despite repeated failure.

"There's no alternative but death and failure."

Imagine flying a plane by yourself with only five sandwiches, a rubber raft, and a few other odds and ends by your side. On top of this, imagine attempting to be the first person to fly solo across the Atlantic. You know that others have tried it and failed—six to be exact—and none survived.

Charles Lindberg set out to do what no one else had done. He took a seat in his wicker chair and took off from Long Island for a journey that would make him a legend. Through his flight he fought against treacherous weather conditions. But the most difficult battle came from within. Fatigue was his greatest enemy.

To keep himself awake through what would become a 33-hour trip, he resorted to resting one eye at a time, using his thumbs to keep his eyelids from sagging, and stamping his feet. Ultimately, he took to chanting over and over to keep him going.

He imagined what his partners and biggest supporters would think, if his excuse for not completing the trip was because he was sleepy. He chanted, "There's no alternative but death and failure…there's no alternative but death and failure," and pushed himself forward.

Lindberg accomplished his goal. Not by listening to the skeptics around him. Or by thinking about the six people who died before him. He succeeded by using his most powerful resource—his desire to succeed—to set a goal and do whatever it took to accomplish it.

What Hollywood Has to Say About Perseverance

The Edge illustrates exactly what kind of person you need to be…and not be. If you haven't seen it, you should. In the film, Anthony Hopkins, Alec Baldwin, and Harold Perrineau play three people who are stranded in the wilderness after their plane crashes.

In the dense forests of Alaska, they have no resources with them and they have no idea where they are. It is wintertime and as they scramble to find their way to safety, they realize that a bear is in pursuit of them. In one scene, we see the bear tear Stephen (Harold Perrineau) to shreds leaving Charles Morse (played by Hopkins) and Robert Green (played by Baldwin) to fend for themselves.

Robert panics. His plane has crashed, he is lost in the mountains in the dead of winter, and a bear whose goal is to kill them has just slaughtered his friend. He constantly dwells on his hopeless circumstances and he fears his future.

Charles, on the other hand, is the exact opposite. He doesn't linger over how dire the situation is. Instead, he focuses on moving ahead and never stopping. In his resourceful state, he devises a plan—to kill the bear before it kills them.

During another scene a rescue helicopter flies overhead. The two run toward it—arms waving in the air and voices calling out to it. Unfortunately, the helicopter does not spot them and it leaves them behind. Feeling helpless, Robert falls to the ground and begins to cry. He is stuck in a state of desperation.

At that moment Charles asks him, "Did you know that you can make fire from ice?"

Why would he ask such a ridiculous question? Because Charles sees that Robert is not in a resourceful state. He wants to pull him out of his desperation to get him thinking about survival.

Robert responds to Charles's optimism with resentment. He wants to remain hopeless. Eventually, however, he realizes that his survival depends on his ability to focus.

He pulls himself together and says, "Alright. Alright. Fire from ice. Let's have it." Charles then explains that you take the ice in your hands and mold it into a lens. Then you use it to concentrate the sunlight on an area to create a fire. Charles knows that the answer to this question is not going to save them. But he understands that their survival depends on maintaining a continually resourceful state.

"What one person can do, another can do."

In one scene, when Robert doubts that the two can kill the bear before it kills them, Charles gets him to chant over and over, "what one man can do another can do…what one man can do another can do"—people have killed bears in the past with spears and knives and they can too.

When you are at a low point in establishing your referral-based business you probably will feel like Robert. I know that while starting my career many times I felt anxiety and fear. But when times are rough, when you don't know how things are going to turn out, and the bills are piling on your desk, this is when your attitude counts most.

The mindset that Charles had in the film is exactly what you need. To understand that "what one person can do another can do" and believing it, will separate you from the rest. It's the difference between someone who goes back to a 9-to-5 job because of a fear of failure and someone who goes on to create a successful referral-based business.

When you are feeling hopeless, do what you need to get your mind off the problem. Think only about results. *Live and breathe inspiration.* At night, when I felt the anxiety of my family counting on me to pay the bills and I was uncertain about myself, I completely immersed myself in movies like

The Edge, Jerry Mac Guire, Men of Honor, Braveheart, and Gladiator.

During the day I listened to CD's that motivated me to work hard. I made CD's that contained music that inspired me to move ahead.

Movies like the ones I listed may not inspire you. The point is to find out what does. Determine what gets you into the most productive state. It may be a film, a song, or a memory you recall when you felt like everything was going your way. Think about what motivates you to achieve. Then when you are frustrated, these movies, memories, songs, or whatever you decide, will help you reach your goals.

Staying the Course

The service you provide may not be one that someone needs everyday. But when you set out to improve the lives of your clients, friends, and family, you leave a lasting impression.

For example, if someone owns a successful coffee house, what keeps his customers coming back versus going to other coffee houses? Each of his customers appreciates being greeted by name and having the coffee prepared exactly the way she wants without even asking. These services reflect how the owner values the relationship with his customers.

The same is true for your referral-based business. Not everyone will need the product or service you offer. But at some point their friends or family will. And when they do, you're business card will come out of their wallet, your name will be mentioned, and your reputation will spread.

For the millions of Americans who want to lose weight the

formula is no secret: Eat right, exercise regularly, and stick with a routine. The keys to a successful referral-based business are just as simple: put the relationship first, maintain contact, and stay the course. Over the years, the more friends you have, the more contacts you make, the more successful you'll be.

When I set out on my own, I didn't have the skills and knowledge I do today. There were no books that lead me through the process of setting up my own business. I hope that the lessons in this book, which reflect everything that I've learned along the way, will guide you in reaching your goals. Best wishes in your journey to join the growing number of people who love working for themselves.

Quick Order Form

Fax orders: 310-370-3011 (fax this form)

Telephone orders: call Beach Lending 310-370-3040. Have your credit card ready.

Order online: www.biznetclub.com/books

Postal orders: 2701 190th. St, Suite #204
Redondo Beach CA 90278
USA
(Send this form)

Name

____

Address

____

City

____

State/Zip

___________/___________

Telephone

____

e-mail address

____

Sales tax (please add 7.75% for books mailed to California addresses)

Delivery by mail
US $4.00 for first book and $2.00 for each additional book
International $9.00 for first book; $5.00 for each additional book

Payment: ❑ Check ❑ Credit Card:
❑ Visa ❑ MasterCard ❑ Optima ❑ Amex ❑ Discover

Card number: ______________________________________
Name on card: ____________________ Exp. date (m/y) _____

The Business Success Club: Connect, Grow, and Build Your Business

Getting the business results you want can be elusive until you make the right connections. Then, it's as easy as flipping a switch.

At the Business Success Club, you don't compete for referrals because in each group we limit membership to one person, per profession.

The Business Success Club is more than an opportunity to network. It's your opportunity to become part of a team of top business professionals and entrepreneurs like you.

We meet for breakfast or lunch once a week to network, share leads, and utilize the group's wealth of resources. Most of all, we provide a framework of support to share ideas and help members with expert guidance.

We are growing everyday and positions fill fast so log onto www.biznetclub.com.